Nursery Rhymes and More
By International Award-Winning Poet
Paula Goldsmith

Nursery Rhymes and More
By International Award-Winning Poet
Paula Goldsmith

Written By: Paula Goldsmith

Copyright By: Paula Goldsmith

Illustrated By: Paula Goldsmith

Nursery Rhymes and More
By International Award-Winning Poet
Paula Goldsmith

Dear Reader,

I hope you will enjoy these fun "Nursery Rhymes and More" poems. Many of my readers have been asking me to publish a book of my Award-Winning Nursery Rhymes. This book "Nursery Rhymes and More" was born. I say, a book is born because of the time, work, tears and pain it takes to publish a book. Just like having a baby.

At the bottom of each poem will be listed what the poem won. This unique book "Nursery Rhymes and More By International Award-Winning Poet Paula Goldsmith" is a Fun book for Ages 2 to 110. In the back of the book, you will find a place to try writing your poems. If you prefer you can journal about life. Make sure you bring your book to life with color This book makes a Great Gift throughout the year. I hope you will enjoy this fun book and will pass it on to others to enjoy.
"Please," Check Out: www.PaulasStories.com

I have been Honored to have my poems chosen to be printed in International Books of Poetry. In 2020 my poem, "When I Was Young" was Featured in "PS: It's Poetry A Brilliant Poetry Anthology Book." An International Book of Poems By International Poets. In 2021 a Children's Book, "Nursery Rhymes & Stories from Poets Around the World," was written by many International writers. I had "five" of my Nursery Rhymes chosen for this wonderful International Children's Book. In 2022 I had three poems chosen for this amazing book, "PS: It's Poetry A Brilliant Poetry Anthology Book Volume ll."

Make sure you check out the back of this book.
Now off to read "Nursery Rhymes and More." Enjoy, Paula

~ Reviews ~

1. Glad to see a book of your Nursery Rhymes.
I love all your amazing books. Very Creative.
From A Reader

2. Another fun book with great poems.
From A Writer

3. I love to take your books when I travel.
I journal about my trip. Great Keepsake.
From A Traveler

4. I have and love all your books.
Keep Writing.
From A Reader

5. Paula, this book will make a
great gift.
From A Writer

6. My kids love your books.
I love this book.
From A Traveler

~ Interview ~

1. Paula, What made you write this Nursery Rhyme book?

*I wrote, "Award-Winning Poems By International Poet
Paula Goldsmith" for adults. Ages 10 to 110. I felt there should
be a special book for the children. Ages 2 to 110.*

2. Congratulations on your new book. How did you come up with
such a mixture of styles in your poems?

*Thank You.... Three international poetry books have my poems
in them.
One of the books is a Nursery Rhyme book for children.*

3. Will, you continue to write books about your poems?

*Great question......... At this time, I do not have an
answer for you. I need more time to publish what
I write, both books and poems.*

4. A novel. What a change for you.
What is this new novel book about?

*Yes, "The Little Wooden Man" is a complete change.........
It is a fun mystery novel. Can the reader solve the mystery
first??? Great reviews have landed on this book
and that makes me very happy.*

5. What is next for you?

*I honestly do not know. I love to write. My readers
can read my "Free" E-Books and my "Free" Poems
on my Website.* www.PaulasStories.com *Enjoy.......*

Print Your Personalized Message Below.
Say What you Want To Say.
Happy Birthday~Get Well~I Love You
Happy Mother's Day……..

In poetry, you will find many different styles/types of poems. Below, you will find a number of these different styles/types of poems. Each poem will have the style/type of poem listed with it.

Acrostic: The first letter in each word on each line will make up a word, phrase, name, topic. You can read this word, phrase, or name vertically (down). The first letter on each line should be capitalized. Some poets make this first letter on each line Bold. More than one word can be used.

Acrostic Rhyme: This style/type starts above. The last word on each line will rhyme. The meter for the rhyme may be different for each rhyme poem. AABBCC. All of the A's will rhyme. All of the B's will rhyme. All of the C's will rhyme. It is up to the poet on how they want the poem to rhyme.

Couplet: Pairs of rhyming lines that are similar in length. Each of the two lines will rhyme. Write two lines then skip a line before the next two lines.

Dramatic Monologue: Only one person/character speaks. The reader is the listener. It can be a short or a long poem. You may want to ask yourself who is this person/character and what are they saying?

Dramatic Verse: This poem tells a story/tale. It is written to be spoken. The poet is talking to you in their words.

Footle: A two-line poem with two syllables in each line. As a rule, it is light/funny. This can be hard to write with only two lines and with two syllables on each line. The writer needs creativity to get their point made.

Free Verse: This poem does not follow a specific meter. No specific rhyme here. A person/poet will pause as they were talking to another person. The poet can express themselves through their words/writing and not through specific meters. The poet can choose their words freely as they express their thoughts to the reader.

Grook: A grook poem can be funny, meaningful, bitter or a combination of feelings. Many times short. Can be a rhyme.

Haibun: First a title is needed followed by a prose-like paragraph. Then ending with a haiku.

Haiku: A Haiku has a total of seventeen syllables. Three lines with 5-7-5 syllables. Haiku is a Japanese word. Few words to express feelings/emotions.

Kimo: This one has three lines with a 10-7-6 syllable count. It will not rhyme. It will have a range between 6, 7 or 10 syllable count on each line.

Limerick: Has five lines. The first, second, and fifth lines have 7 to 10 syllables and rhyme. Lines three and four have 5 to 7 syllables and also rhyme with each other.

List: Just as the name says. A list is a list of things, people, places etc.… It may or may not rhyme. This has a start and an end like a story.

Monoku: One single line with seventeen syllables makes up this poem. You will find the letter of the first word is a capital letter followed by all small letters. As in speech where will be a pause.

Ninette: Has nine lines. The first line has a one-word syllable. Each line increase by one syllable. At the midpoint start decreasing back down to a one-word syllable.

Nursery Rhyme: These poems are written with children in mind. The last words of each line will rhyme. The meter for the rhyme may be different for each rhyme poem. AABBCC. All of the A's will rhyme. All of the B's will rhyme. All of the C's will rhyme. It is up to the poet how they want the poem to rhyme.

Ode: It is centered around something the writer wishes to praise. For example, their spouse, dog/cat.

Personification: Puts life into inanimate objects. These things will be described as having thoughts and or emotions the way a human being would. A Personification can be used to make a point and or thought so the reader can understand better what the poet is telling them.

Pleiades: Seven lines with each line starting with the same letter as the title. Only one word is allowed for the title.

Quatrain: Four lines are written. Lines 2 and 4 must rhyme. Lines 2 and 4 must also have a similar number of syllables. It may have more than one stanza.

Rhyme: A rhyming poem has the last word on each line rhyme. The meter for the rhyme may be different for each rhyme poem. AABBCC. All of the A's will rhyme. All of the B's will rhyme. All of the C's will rhyme. It is up to the poet how they want the poem to rhyme.

Shape: The poet's words will form a shape. These can be hard to write. Making the letters/words form a shape. They are fun to see and to read.

Tanka: Is a short poem, similar to a Haiku. Deep purpose, meaning, and give the readers a strong feeling. Five lines with 5-7-5-7-7 syllables.

Tetractys: Five lines of 1, 2, 3, 4, 10 syllables. A total of 20 syllables. Then you can reverse it back. Five lines of 10, 4, 3, 2, 1 syllables. For a total of 40 syllables.

Verse: This one does not have a set meter. It flows freely as the poet writes it. They are sometimes identified as stanza poems.

~ Table Of Contents ~

38. Little Green Frog Nursery Rhyme
39. Big Blue
40. The Butterfly of Many Colors
41. Good Better Best
42. I Am Stuck In A Christmas Globe
43. Smile Stand Select
44. Brother
45. I Am In A Pickle With You
46. A Happy Birthday Dream
47. Wild Country Bears
48. I Will Never Forget My Aunt
49. FUNTIMES BIRTHDAY
50. Strawberry Ice Cream
51. Flowers
52. Mother's Day
53. Zoom Santa
54. Santa's Reindeer
55. Ants
56. Ice Lake
57. Shape
58. Violets Are Blue
59. Spring Is In The Air
60. Time
61. A Lovely Day
62. The Night Sky
63. Spring Is Coming Soon
64. A Poem Lovely As A Garden

My Flower Garden Nursery Rhyme

My pretty pink flowers have been crowned,
big yellow bees went round and round.
Pretty flowers of all colors cover the green ground,
the blue and orange butterflies are all-around.
The red birds make a lovely tweet~tweet sound,
you can hear them singing in the background.

Date Written: 4/16/2022
1 Place ~ Nursery Rhyme

Big Brown Bear

big strong furry brown
fishing for salmon with paws~
prancing through flowers

Date Written: 4/12/2022
3 Place ~ Haiku

Spring Is In The Air

Beautiful birds are singing to me
high up in the trees with a big bee
bending to pick some flowers
my buns shown like towers
they were hanging out for all to see

Date Written: 2/18/2022
4 Place ~ Limerick

Blue Dinosaur

Little friend of mine, we have such a wonderful time.
Everyone is so afraid of you, even if you are just made of blue.
We play all day and night, then we can sleep so tight.
In our dreams we play until we awake,
then we go running down and play at the lake.
Before you know it the day is done,
then there is no more fun.
Now it is time to sleep again,
so mommy can write our thoughts with a pen.

Date Written: 7/27/2019
Honorable Mention ~ Free Verse

Sleepy Time Nursery Rhyme

It is sleepy time little one,
today, all your playing is now done.
Tomorrow you will have more fun,
you will be up early like the big yellow sun.
You and puppy can play and run,
you may even make a home run.

Date Written: 4/19/2021
1 Place ~ Nursery Rhyme

If I Were Your Brother,
Boy Would You Be In Trouble

I asked where is my bag of candy?
With a sheepish face you said,
the dog ate it What dog?
We do not have a dog.
Oh!
Spot my furry and hungry little stuffed dog.
If I were your brother,
boy would you be in trouble.
How can I get upset with a story like Spot?
I hope Spot did not get sick eating all of my candy.
With that,
one very sick little boy ran for the bathroom.
Guess Spot ate way too much of my candy.
I never had to tell Mom and Dad.
Funny,
I never lost my bag of candy again.

Date Written:10/27/2019
Second Place ~ Free Verse

My Secret November Twinkle Fairy

Under a tree I sat enjoying the beautiful day,
a breeze in my hair, birds singing sweetly,
butterflies fluttering from flower to flower.
What did I see?

Are my eyes deceiving me?
Among the brilliant fall leaves and flowers,
a movement I see but not a leaf.
A Twinkle Fairy could it be?

No, they are only in stories you read.
I must have dosed off,
was I dreaming or was it all real?
As I walked away I turned for one last look
at the brilliant fall leaves and flowers,
a little Twinkle Fairy was waving back at me.

Date Written:11/3/2019
2 Place ~ Free Verse

Teddy Bear Cuz Nursery Rhyme

My best friend my Teddy Bear Cuz,
he loved honey and watch out for the buzz.
Honey is sweet for the bees,
honey is sweet for me.
Teddy Bear Cuz almost got stung,
mommy said "watch out for your tongue."
Teddy Bear Cuz was so funny,
he wants to catch and rub bunny.
My best friend my Teddy Bear Cuz,
we will nap and sleep as the bees buzz.
Dreaming of big pots of honey,
we can eat until we have a full tummy.

Date Written: 3/12/2021
1 Place ~ Nursery Rhyme
Note: This Is A New Poem. The idea came from my book,
"The Adventures Of Baby Cuz."
Baby Cuz is the little bear's name.

My Favorite Animal Angel

A rescue dog she would be,
her halo was bright for all to see.
She loved her blusher on both cheeks,
the pink color she would seek.
Riding in a car was a huge thrill,
I made it a big deal.
With our seat belts now on,
we were both ready to make the car run.
Night was massage time as we drift off to sleep,
in the morning from the bed we would leap.
Now Angel is gone to heaven to wait,
the rainbow bridge I need to cross has no date.

Date Written:12/24/2019
8 Place ~ Rhyme

Angels Come In All Shapes And Sizes

(This dog was an angel in a fur coat)
Angels come in all shapes and sizes
this one was full of prizes.
An Easter gift, oh!
so soft and not stiff.
Boys got her at the pound,
and she was all smiles and never a frown.
Thirty pounds was all she was,
this angel came with no flaws.
Her perfumed cream colored fur,
would make me want to purr.
Lovingly messaged to sleep each night,
up and out with the morning sunlight.
Daily she sang her song to the rabbits,
this was one of her heavenly habits.
I talked and she listened well,
did she think I was under a spell?
She loved her blusher make up,
it made her rosy cheeks want to jump.
Off in the car we would go,
when we came home she would say oh no.
Her angel kisses,
were always there as was her best wishes.
Heavenly angel I now need to say good bye,
one day I will once again say hi.

Date Written: 2/12/2020
3 Place ~ Rhyme

Rooster Sounding Off

rooster sounding off
all up with the dawn breaking
work must start today

Date Written: 4/26/2020
1 Place ~ Haiku

Butterflies Around

Butterflies around,
angels surround.
Fly little butterfly,
did you just go by.
Fly to the angels near you,
with your wings of blue.
Come near to me,
please do not flee.

Date Written: 3/28/2020
Honorable Mention ~ Rhyme

Butterfly Nursery Rhyme

Beautiful flying butterfly,
come to me and do not be shy.
Your pretty blue color is like the sky,
with the big white clouds up high.
From flower to flower you do fly,
do not leave me or I will cry.
Mommy do I need to say goodbye,
yes, the butterfly needs to go bye-bye.

Date Written: 4/9/2021
2 Place ~ Nursery Rhyme

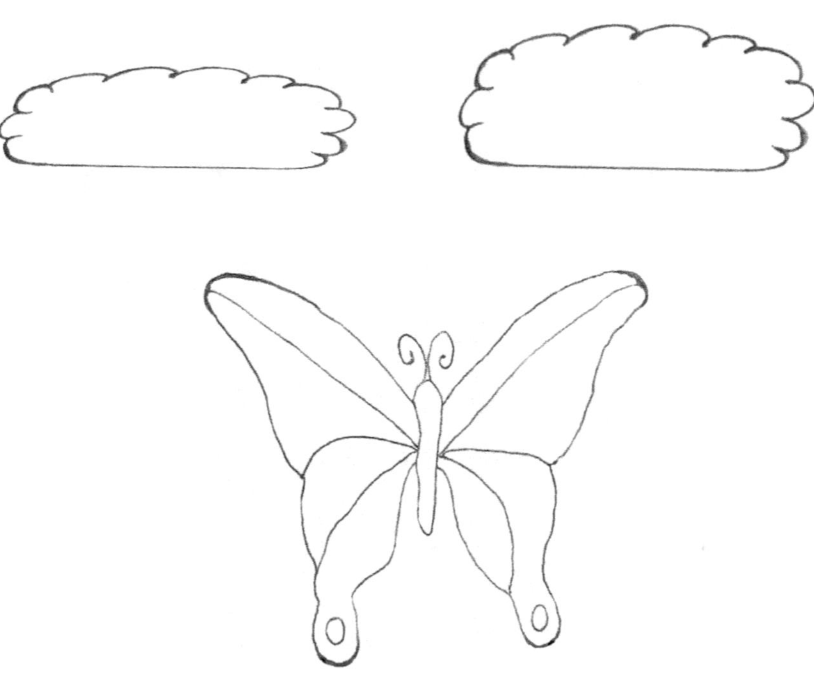

A Sunny Day

A sunny day for you,
a sunny day for me.
A day to say,
I love you.
A day for you to say,
you love me too.

Date Written: 3/31/2020
Honorable Mention ~ Free Verse

My Carousel Horse

When I was three I loved riding my wooden horse,
going round and round would keep me on course.
I would ride him up and then down,
then we would go back around.
When I had children of my own,
my wooden horse was loved by daughter Joan.
She would ride and ride,
with her eyes opened wide.
Now my grandchild loves my wooden horse,
I can hear giddy up in her voice.
Boy how time has blown by,
now I watch my wooden horse and just sigh.

Date Written: 3/18/2020
Honorable Mention ~ Rhyme

Why Did The Cat Leave Home

Why did the cat leave home,
so he could roam.
Under the porch he did sleep,
it was cool and it was cheap.
In "my private universe" he would wish,
he could eat buckets of fresh fish.

Date Written: 9/10/2020
Honorable Mention ~ Rhyme

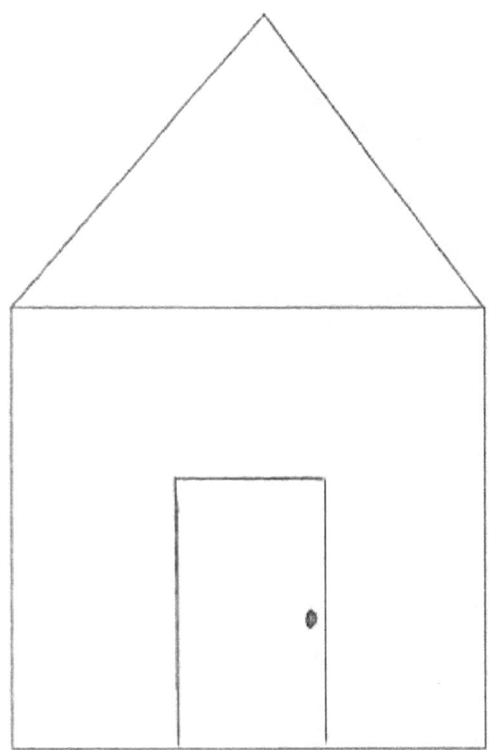

My Kitten Nursery Rhyme

I hold my soft kitten tight,
we will sleep through the night.
Dreams of you and me with a big red kite,
we will run in mom's garden before the morning light.
The yellow sun is coming up bright,
we must get out of sight.

Date Written: 10/8/2021
Honorable Mention ~ Nursery Rhyme

EAT

EAT
sugar
beautiful
warm from her oven
wonderful memories
my grandma's Christmas cookies
"my full tummy with lots of love"

Date Written: 9/9/2020
1 Place ~ Verse

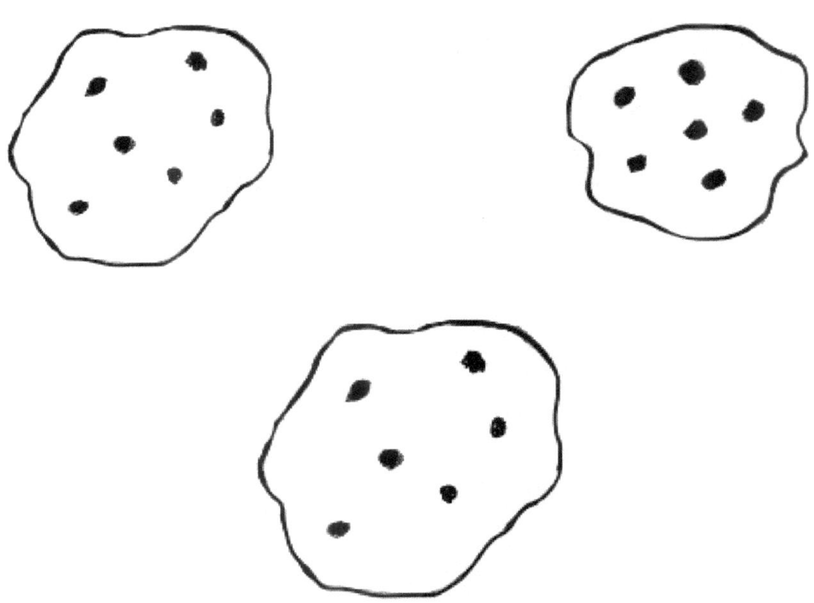

Bear and Me

Bear and me, as lonely as can be.
We want to play with thee,
now we are two and not three.
Angels have one more,
heaven has opened it's door.
Bear and me here we are,
wishing upon a star.

Date Written: 8/24/2020
12 Place ~ Rhyme

Buzzing Little Bees

buzzing little bees
make some sweet honey for me
buzz from rose to rose

Date Written: 8/17/2020
6 Place ~ Haiku

Jellyfish And Me

Young kids enjoy playing in the yard,
until the dock called out come over here.
Alluring water caught their eyes,
white shining somethings are swimming by.
What could they be we all called out,
jellyfish was the adult reply.
We watched as they swim closer and closer,
then I found myself in the water with them.
My friends had pushed me in,
so funny they thought it would be to take a swim.
A big strong hand I did find,
like always my daddy to my rescue.
Inflicted with immediate itching and scratching,
now the crying began.
Off to the bathtub I was pulled,
baking soda bath then wrapped in greasy lotion.
Itching and scratching for days to come, all the so call friends are
now gone.

Date Written: 8/6/2020
2 Place ~ Free Verse
Note: A true story.................

Butterflies

pretty butterflies
wings painted many colors
fly to each flower

Date Written 8/3/2020
1 Place ~ Haiku

Red Bird

I am a red bird sitting in a huge oak tree,
hiding in the leaves so you cannot see me.
I am fluttering my pretty red feathers,
they keep me warm no need for a sweater.
The chicks keep me very busy,
some days it makes me dizzy.
They need to be fed again,
this is a real pain.
Off to get cleaned in that birdbath,
watch out there is a cat on the path.
I love flying around,
I can cover a lot of ground.
Little ones tucked in the nest,
I can finally get some rest.
A mother's job is never done,
All mother's work from sun to sun.

Date Written: 7/17/2020
2 Place ~ Personification

Parakeet

When I was in third grade.
I came to your aid.
A sick teacher's dad,
made his parakeet so very sad.
My teacher asked,
would I take the parakeet fast.
I needed to ask my mom,
sure hope she will not go off like a bomb.
My parents may put me in a handcuff,
because I could not say yes fast enough.

Date Written: 7/9/2020
5 Place ~ Rhyme

Little Green Frog Nursery Rhyme

Little green frog so sweet to me,
look up there is a big yellow bee.
The big yellow bee is singing,
here we are grinning.

Date Written: 3/22/2021
2 Place ~ Nursery Rhyme

Big Blue

Oh, big ocean blue below just like the big blue sky above.
Many amazing shades of blues you can see from near to far.
With white fluffy foam on the water below and
white fluffy clouds above.
The changing big ocean blue and the changing blue
in the big sky from dawn to dusk.
May I always see and enjoy the many
amazing shades of blues from near to far.
What a sight you both are to see from dawn to dusk.
Oh, big ocean blue below just like the big blue sky above.

Date Written: 6/6/2019
1 Place ~ Free Verse

The Butterfly of Many Colors

My little butterfly filled with colors from the rainbow.
The glittering colors from reds to blues to
yellows to greens to orange.
You flutter from near to far.
From one flower to another and to
another flower you flutter.
I wish, I could fly away with you.
From one flower to another and to another flower
we could flutter the day away together.
The sunlight changes the glittering rainbow
colors on your fragile wings.
Your wings that look like beautiful stained glass.
I wish, I could fly away with you.
Far, far away we could fly and
see the glittering rainbow world together.

Date Written: 6/7/2019
3 Place ~ Free Verse

Good Better Best

Great
Old
Ornery
Dads

Bless
Every
Toddler
Today
Each
Rising

Before
Evening
Sunset
Tonight

Date Written: 9/29/2019
2 Place ~ Acrostics

I Am Stuck In A Christmas Globe

I Am Stuck in a Christmas Globe for all to see,
I stand here patiently.
Here I am looking at you,
you just pass me by without a glance.
I cannot move in my snowy world,
yet you are warm and toasty all the time.
Now and then you shake me up,
then the snow falls heavily.
I once again get covered with snow,
all white and cold I just stand and wait.

Date Written:11/29/2019
3Place ~ Free Verse

Smile Stand Select

Why look so sad?
I want to make you smile.
I make funny,
I make you laugh with what I say.
See you have a beautiful smile shining brightly.
I make funny,
I make you laugh with what I say.
I now can see a light in your eyes like glittering diamonds.
I make funny,
I make you laugh with what I say.
I want to brighten up your day.
Make your heavy load lighter if only for a moment.
I make funny,
I make you laugh with what I say.
It is all about making you smile today.
Let's all make funny with what we say
and put a smile on some ones face.

Date Written: 12/31/2019
Honorable Mention ~ Free Verse
(For many years, I have said, "I make funny,
I make you laugh with what I say."
I love to see people smile.)

Brother

Brother you were the boy that grew into a great man.
Running cars were your joy.
Offering advice was your line.
The day you passed I was left alone.
Heaven now has one more angel.
Eternally you will be missed.
Recognized for our strong resemblance.

Date Written:1/12/2020
1 Place ~ Acrostics

I Am In A Pickle With You

Here we sit all cold and wet,
please do not start to fret.
Let me snuggle up to you,
I promise not to chew.
I think these new glass jars,
really came in a box from mars.
Some say this stinky pickle juice,
tastes like it came from a big moose.
I don't care if you're sweet or dill,
you will always be my thrill.
We both may be green,
so we can't help our jeans.
I will love you until the end,
you will always be my best friend.
Guess we can't get out of this pickle we are in,
so let's just say amen.

Date Written: 2/16/2020
3 Place ~ Rhyme
(Two talking pickles stuck in a jar.)

A Happy Birthday Dream

Happy Birthday, it comes each May.
Tonight I will dream,
of a beautiful cake with ice cream.
I hope there will be many gifts each with a card,
maybe enough to fill my backyard.

Date Written: 4/7/2020
Honorable Mention ~ Rhyme

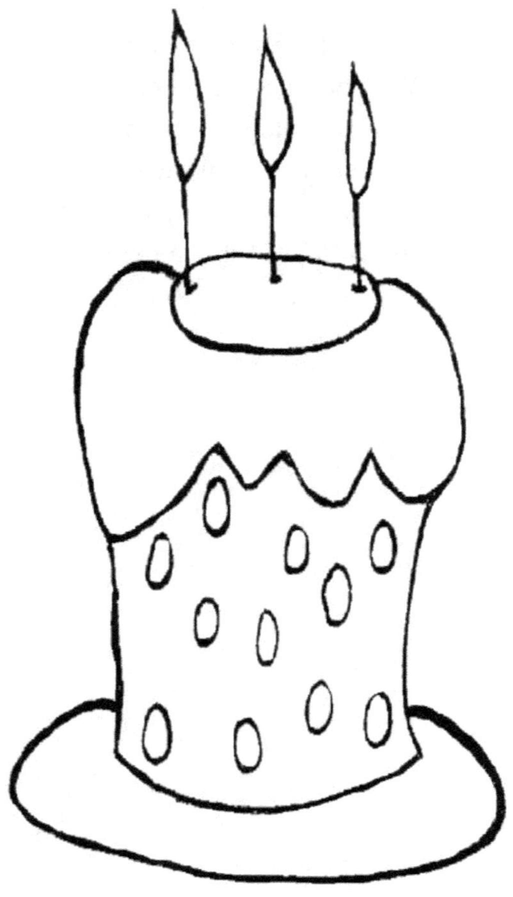

Wild Country Bears

I went for a walk and what did I see,
bears over there looking at me.
My mind did a flash,
Oh! bears don't eat me.
I am tough as can be,
I am way too old for thee.

Date Written: 4/7/2020
Honorable Mention ~ Free Verse

I Will Never Forget My Aunt

I will never forget my aunt:
Your big smile that when on for miles.
How you creamed your velvet skin each night.
The coconut cake that was to die for.
How we would laugh until we cried.
Riding the bus into town for shopping and lunch.
A special small box each Christmas with that five inside.
Up early to go crabbing and cooking for lunch.
Loved talking with you on the phone from miles away.
How I cried when I would go home and leave you behind.
I prayed you had been my mom so I could stay.
To this day I miss you more than words can say.

Date Written: 5/11/2020
2 Place ~ Free Verse

FUNTIMES BIRTHDAY

Fun today let's get some gru**B**
Under the tree we sat just you and *I*
Now we can be a pai**R**
This day was a great even**T**
I will go walk on the beac**H**
My gift was in my car**D**
Enjoyment was abound in the are**A**
See today it is my birthda**Y**

Date Written: 5/27/2020
3 Place ~ Double Acrostic~ Reading Down.
The First Letter on Each Line Forms A word. The Last Letter on
Each Line Forms A word. This Is Hard To Write.

Strawberry Ice Cream

Dish held my sugar cone
Ice cream of plump strawberries they were not alone
Sunny afternoon this was sweet when I was young
Hushed my talking tongue.

Date Written: 6/19/2022
1 Place ~ Acrostic

Flowers

Today you sent
me beautiful flowers
because
you love me.

Date Written: 5/8/2022
1 Place ~ Verse

Mother's Day

This little one you were given,
from God above with grace and love.
Young and with little help what were you to do,
rocking and crying the days turned into years.
God heard your many prayers for your many children,
now all grown they were heaven sent.

Date Written: 5/2/2022
Honorable Mention ~ Free Verse

Zoom Santa

After last year~after all the millions of miles,
Santa put his sled in for a check-up with smiles.
Last year the sled was very slow,
it needed a lot more go~go.
He wants to make sure all the girls~boys,
will get all of their many toys.
His mechanic said~take it for a ride,
Santa came back and cried.
His sled now has plenty of Zoom,
out the back came a huge fiery plume.
Santa had a jolly big laugh,
a million thanks to all of your staff.

Date Written: 12/5/2021
2 Place ~ Rhyme

Santa's Reindeer

The reindeer said the hay did not agree,
their stomach had a huge bee.
A diaper they would need,
they all wanted no more feed.
Santa was changing diapers on one knee.

Date Written: 12/13/2021
9 Place ~ Limerick

Ants

Ants work like busy little bees,
pilling sand up in the breeze.
They work with great ease,
are they on their knees.
Even when there is a freeze,
the ants are out under the trees.
Building a house to store their cheese,
I guess their door has very small keys.
I would love to come in Louise,
can I if I say pretty please.

Date Written: 1/15/2022
1 Place ~ Rhyme

Ice Lake

my ice covered lake
skating~hockey~ice fishing
fun for young and old

Date Written: 1/16/2022
6 Place ~ Haiku

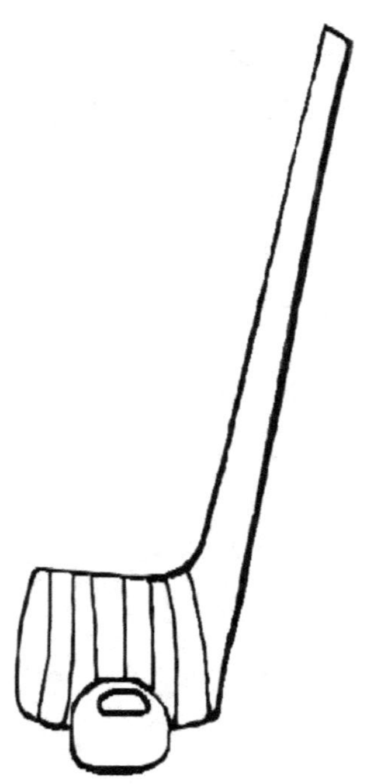

Shape

See the form in writing
Size does not matter here
Shapes you create for fun
Specific shape effect
Show your freedom to all
Something very special
Spaces tell a story

Date Written:1/20/2022
3 Place ~ Pleiades

Violets Are Blue

Violets in blue
you say they match my two eyes
blue eyes are crying
I wish you were here with me
a card is all I can hold

Date Written: 2/8/2022
2 Place ~ Tanka

Spring Is In The Air

Beautiful birds are singing to me
high up in the trees with a big bee
bending to pick some flowers
my buns shown like towers
they were hanging out for all to see

Date Written: 2/18/2022
4 Place ~ Limerick

Time

Time is a funny thing.
When we want it to go~it stays, like pain.
When we want it to stay like a vacation, it goes.
Time is a funny thing.

Date Written: 2/22/2022
Honorable Mention ~ Free Verse

A Lovely Day

The bright sun was peeking through the curtain,
I opened it up wide to let the light in.
In the trees the birds are singing,
singing songs just to me.
Oh what a pretty day,
they are singing away.
Dressed and outside I will go,
my garden awaits with a glow.
The flowers with their perfume smell,
now calling bees and butterflies from everywhere.
I sit sipping my cup of coffee,
as I watch the beauty of this day.

Date Written: 2/23/2022
3 Place ~ Free Verse

The Night Sky

As the sun is getting ready to go to bed,
where will it lay it's head.
The light will now shed,
for darkness needs to spread.
The pretty night sky,
makes me want to cry.
Can you hear the full moon,
is it playing a love tune.
The twinkling far off stars,
I wonder if they really go to mars.
The stars look like diamonds across the many acres,
could their beauty be for matchmakers.
For the beauty one cannot buy,
it will make me want to just sigh.

Date Written: 2/25/2022
2 Place ~ Rhyme

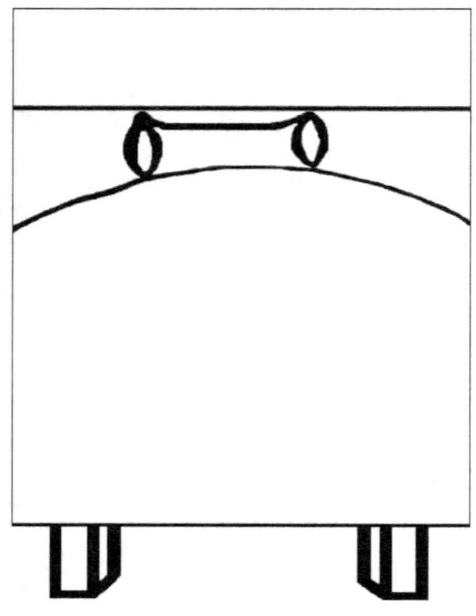

Spring Is Coming Soon

Flower pots will be cracking
Winter will be packing
Spring has sprung
The bells have rung

Date Written: 2/28/2022
3 Place ~ Grook

A Poem Lovely As A Garden

My beautiful spring fresh flowers,
Budding after a rain showers.
Pretty butterflies are flying,
Flower to flower are spying.
The fountain was filled with water,
Did I see a swimming otter.
All the tall green weeds I must pull,
Now I have another bagful.
I am so tried and very hot,
All flowers are out of each pot.
Time to rest with a cup of tea,
Watch out here comes a yellow bee.

Date Written: 3/1/2022
Honorable Mention ~ Couplet

My Red Birds

My red birds sitting in a tree,
I hear them singing just to me.
The two look so in love,
a big nest they are building.
Many little ones they will be having,
each day a new baby is chirping.
The babies need to learn to sing,
to fly as mom pushes them out.
Babies are now flying on their own,
Spring is here for my red birds.

Date Written: 3/9/2022
3 Place ~ Imagism

My Cardinal

my cardinal bird
singing sweetly just to me~
now eating your seed

Date Written: 3/15/2022
6 Place ~ Haiku

My Black Cat

Did you know,
cats are smart.
Black cats are extra smart,
with a sixth sense.
We know to stay off the streets,
black cats on the streets mean trouble for people.
Black cats need extra love and rubs,
we are very independent.
Don't disturb us while napping or sleeping,
you will get a huge hiss.
We love play time,
we need plenty of toys and catnip for us to enjoy.
Make sure our litter box is changed each day,
we like nice smells around us.
Remember black cats need extra rubs,
it's time for some of those extra rubs.

Date Written: 3/22/2022
1 Place ~ Dramatic Monologue

Baby Girl

It is a beautiful spring morning,
a baby girl has been born.
She is wrapped in a pink blanket~it is so warming,
she is wrapped in love by her parents~sound a horn.
As she grows and plays,
she will learn the weight of the world is on
her shoulders in many ways.
She will have many goals in life,
one could be as a wife.
She may want to be a doctor~astronaut~
teacher~world leader,
it will all be up to her even as a lip reader.
A mother and her firstborn,
with many little ones of her own to raise.
Today on this beautiful spring morning a baby girl was born,
tomorrow the sky will be her's to own and blaze.

Date Written: 3/23/2022
2 Place ~ Ode

Big Bees

Springs pretty colors are here
The big bees are buzzing near
So do not have any fear
I will keep you safe from the bees dear

Date Written: 4/4/2022
9 Place ~ Rhyme

Singing Butterfly

I am a butterfly that loves to sing,
every note and word I do fling,
to rhythm I do cling,
music by the flowers has a beat and ring,
the ladybugs threw kisses with love.
Big Green likes to join in,
his deep frog voice comes with a big grin,
our sounds will make you spin,
we like to play outside of the inn,
they say our voices fit like a glove.
Rose is a backup voice,
then there is sweet pea Joyce,
take both and do not make a choice,
with the four of us we can now rejoice,
is this called garden music~kind of.
We play and sing all night long,
the flowers like to sing along,
everyone likes to hear tweet~tweet
from the birdsong,
some of the music can get real strong,
in the end it sounds like from heaven above.

Date Written: 4/8/2022
9 Place ~ Rhyme

Winter Wishes

Cold wet winter winds
plenty of snow to play in
snowmen to build ~ sleds.
Hot chocolate to drink up,
soft furry blanket ~ cuddle.

Date Written: 12/2/2021
4 Place ~ Tanka

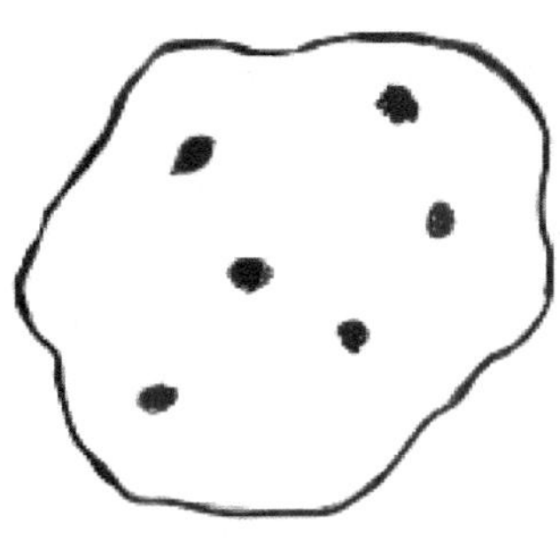

Christmas Gift Memory

I love the huge tree with all it's lights,
the bright colors light up the cold nights.
My aunt's special gift,
always gave me a holiday lift.
A little box was waiting just for me,
every year was $5.00 not a bee.
First year married she went crazy with two gifts each,
my husband had a nightgown of peach.
He had no words~no speech,
for the name tag I did reach.

Date Written:11/30/2021
3 Place ~ Rhyme

How One Paints

In the art galleries of the world,
we find may priceless pieces.
Many are very old from the masters,
many are newer from modern day times.
They have painted in charcoal~oils and watercolors,
today with a knife~their finger~a can of spray paint.
From flowers to the sky in amazing colors,
to a portrait of you and me.
An artist is an artist in their own rite,
painting with their creativity from above.

Date Written:11/8/2021
1 Place ~ Free Verse

Red Beauty

Beauty is your name red apple just for me
Your fruity and lovely taste lasts in my mouth
It's my duty to enjoy and chew you well
My best friend Judy and I will share you
Your skin of red ruby is pretty for all to see

Date Written:11/3/2021
3 Place ~ Rhyme

Thanksgiving Day

Family and friends
table covered~home cooked food
thankful prayer said
smiling~laughing and eating
empty plates~tummies full

Date Written:10/19/2021
1 Place ~ Tanka

The Kitchen

The boiling pot,
sat on the cold stove with a jolt.
All waiting for dinner,
the seven P.M. clock was a winner.
We ate to our fill,
I am so hungry I could kill.
The dishes are all done,
the sink is filled so lets run.

Date Written: 9/8/2021
5 Place ~ Rhyme

Fall

Fall
cooler
days enjoy
apple cider
paint pumpkin faces
colored leaves everywhere
shorter golden sunset
sweaters being worn
squirrels get nuts
pretty mums
apples
red

Date Written: 9/3/2021
2 Place ~ Verse

The Sea

Quote By Poet "The Power Of The Sea and Thee"

When I was little and we went to the beach,
it was early in the morning.
The bright sun would be dancing on the water,
looking as if the blue sea was sprinkled
with a million diamonds.
When the sea was calm my dad would say,
today the sea is as flat as a pancake.
There were times we went out to fish,
seas as calm as could be.
In hours the calm seas were rough as a roller coaster,
not knowing if we would make it back to land.
"The Power Of The Sea and Thee"
Weather be as calm as a pancake,
or rough as a roller coaster.
The one that makes the mighty sea,
He is in me.

Date Written: 8/20/2021
2 Place ~ Dramatic Verse

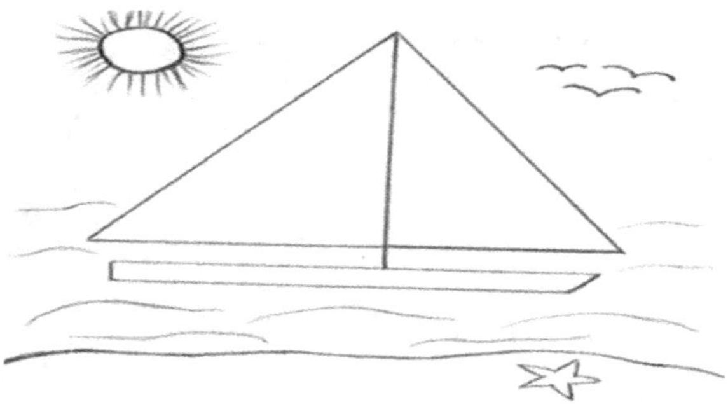

My Sky

When I saw the yellow sunrise,
I could not believe my eyes.
I looked up to the bright pretty sky,
I saw you looking back and I wanted to cry.
With a pretty background of blue,
Big fluffy white clouds are everywhere.
I see many shapes even a cute little bear.
As the day now comes to an end,
all your pretty colors will blend.
Your bright sky pink,
just gave me a huge wink.
The deep royal purple color,
made me feel like a real scholar.
The orange tangerine wave,
went throughout the sky I wanted to save.
It was followed by red,
now guess it is time for me to go to bed.

Date Written: 8/17/2021
9 Place ~ Rhyme

Bears

Bears
nursery rhymes
my books
I love you
now sleep
to dream
of you

Date Written: 7/5/2021
3 Place ~ Verse

Big Yellow

Yellow
Bright light
Long days
To play
Sun fun
Get burned
Skin red
Cream skin
Summer
Picnic
Hot grill
Smells good
Eat now
Tree shade
Play sports
Let's swim
Day ends
Sundown

Date Written: 5/29/2021
1 Place ~ Footle

Unicorns

Unicorns all ages
Under my bed hiding
Until I go to sleep
Unbaked cookies we eat
Uncertain fur colors
Unreal-magical
Unpleasant they are gone

Date Written: 4/30/2021
3 Place ~ Pleiades

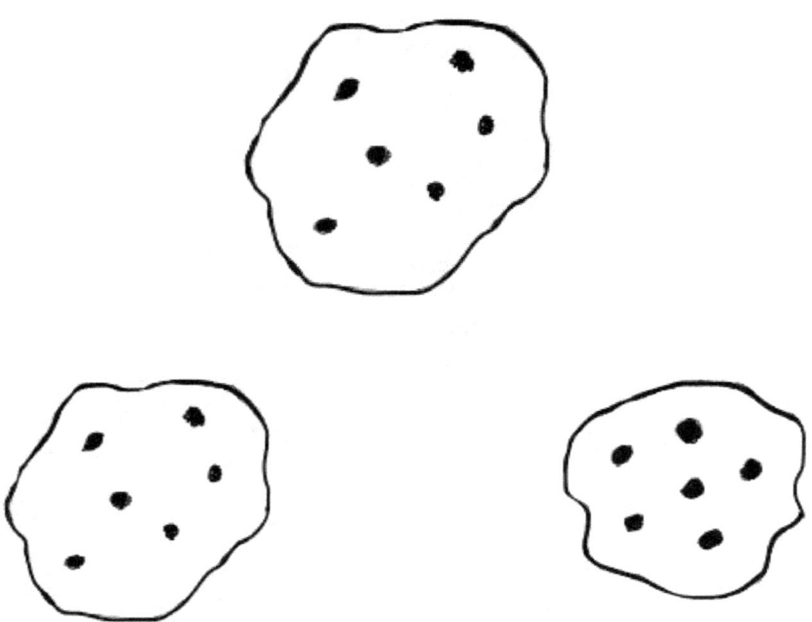

Children Listen More

"Children Listen More"
Quote by Poet Paula Goldsmith

When I was young so very many years ago,
both my parents ruled the house from
morning till night;
their many rules were very clear for you to know,
in life growing up-taking a spouse they were right.
Rules were made by both parents and
were the house laws,
you did not act out and you never did talk back;
like it or not you lived-died by the rules you saw,
your parents were the law and would
give a big smack.
Could not wait for dating since it was a big thrill,
when it came to the clothes to wear and to the men;
best look and act like a lady or dad will kill,
son you are told you better have her home by ten.
Oh my-all parents rules were meant to be followed,
parents need to have rules-children to listen more;
today's children's heads seem to be empty-hollowed,
children yelling and acting like a raging boar.
When I was young so very many years ago,
rules were made by both parents and
were the house laws;
could not wait for dating since it was a big thrill,
oh my-all parents rules were meant to be followed.

Date Written:12/6/2020
3 Place ~Rhyme

A Little Jewelry Box

As a very young child,
the little jewelry box was just for me.
My loving aunt had a box filled with her love,
beautifully gift wrapped and mailed to me.
All year I waited for her loving box,
I always opened it with a surprise.
I always knew what was inside,
a new five dollar bill was waiting for me.
This little jewelry box filled-wrapped
with her love,
meant more to me than the whole world.
She lived so very far away,
I did not see her very often.
With each little jewelry box,
I just knew she was here next to me.
The many miles just disappeared,
her love I could hold dear.
She is now in heaven where she belongs,
I will never forget her little jewelry box
from each year.

Date Written: 3/10/2021
2 Place ~ Dramatic Verse

Santa Said

Elves have been very busy making toys,
all year for the good girls and boys.
Santa sent out a memo,
stop the machines line up in a row.
The deer have been practicing flying again,
just like a real jet plane.
Santa sent an e-mail to the deer,
the look on their faces brought on real fear.
Santa said have you heard,
hot off the press I have the word.
The world has been sick,
with Covid and this is no trick.
The kids cannot be disappointed this year,
so let's go grab our PPE gear.

Date Written:12/7/2020
2 Place ~ Rhyme

Homework Destruction

I was in third grade when I heard a tale,
a tale I cannot believe.
The teacher asked for our homework,
little Susan said my hamster ate it.
I never knew hamsters would eat homework,
Susan got off with a warning.
Next week our homework was due,
the teacher said to put it on her desk.
Little Johnny sat quietly in his seat,
as we all filed by with our papers.
The teacher asked Johnny
where is your paper,
oh my dog ate it.
With an upset look the teacher said,
not original so here is more work for you.
Next week our homework was due,
I had stayed up way too late.
What in the world was I going to do,
I had no paper to turn in.
I stood up and said,
teacher the flaming pterodactyl
ate my homework.
The teacher was laughing so hard,
I think she peed herself and I was off the hook.

Date Written:1/21/2021
3 Place ~ Dramatic Verse

Two Young Boys

Two young boys read about gold and adventure,
this started a life long obsession.
The years went by,
school-jobs and a business to buy.
Gold and adventure would fill their soul,
now these young boys have turned
into men of old.
Still looking for that one huge load,
they went to an island in a far off land.
Many have died here but the story says
one more to go,
then the treasure and adventure will be done.
Could this all be just plain fork lore
or maybe it is all gone,

what year will finish this story-what year
will finish this adventure.
Two young boys still wanting to find
the gold and adventure,
still not ready to give up.

Date Written: 2/28/2021
1 Place ~ Free Verse

Awaken For School

awaken for school-dad is there with hot coffee

Date Written: 2/26/2021
1 Place ~ <u>Monoku</u>
Note: In junior high and high school my dad would
wake me up each school day with a hot cup of coffee.
A dad's loving touch.

Flower Pots

My garden is filled in pots
I have no yard-no lots

I will need beautiful flower seeds
I will need something to kill the weeds

Lots of lovely butterflies to pollinate
Flowers just watch and wait

I need more garden tools
I also need a small stool

My garden needs a sky filled with sun
Big clouds bring the rain for fun

Flowers growing bigger day by day
All planted in pots made out of clay

My garden now very pretty
Come take a look from the city

Date Written: 2/21/2021
2 Place ~ List

My Imagination

My imagination can run wild,
from fairy tales to lions that don't smile.
Can you imagine being in a fairy tale,
where all the knights in armor were for sale.
Can you imagine in my dreams
the lions don't smile,
the lions all got eaten by the crocodiles.
Can you imagine by day-night or a book,
my imagination is always working
and never off the hook.

Date Written: 1/24/2021
4 Place ~ Rhyme

LOVE

Love is kind
On my mind
Very loving
Emotionally stunning

Date Written: 1/14/2021
4 Place ~ Acrostic Rhyme

A-U-T-U-M-N

"A"utumn what a very special time of the year.
"U"nder the tree lay glistening red and orange leaves.
"T"he autumn will not last too long.
"U"naware the squirrels go about finding their nuts.
"M"any apples picked for the pies and cider.
"N"ature will start to hide for the cold winter months.

Date Written:10/18/2020
3 Place ~ Acrostic

Some Friends

Some friends come.
Some friends go.
I am so glad you came and
hope you will never go.

Date Written:10/12/2020
3 Place ~ Verse

Checkers

Checkers what a game,
I do not want to go down in a flame.
You jump me,
then I jump you as fast as can be.
Fun for young and old,
this I have been told.
With coins in black and red,
we can play until one is dead.
Rethink your move,
before I approve.
Win-win-win, did I make your head spin.

Date Written:10/10/2020
2 Place ~ Rhyme

Mathematics

May I show you numbers
Math numbers to add now
Many to subtract from
My coins make me dollars
Mom help me with homework
Minds great and small count twice
Monday no homework yeah

Date Written:10/6/2020
2 Place ~ Pleiades

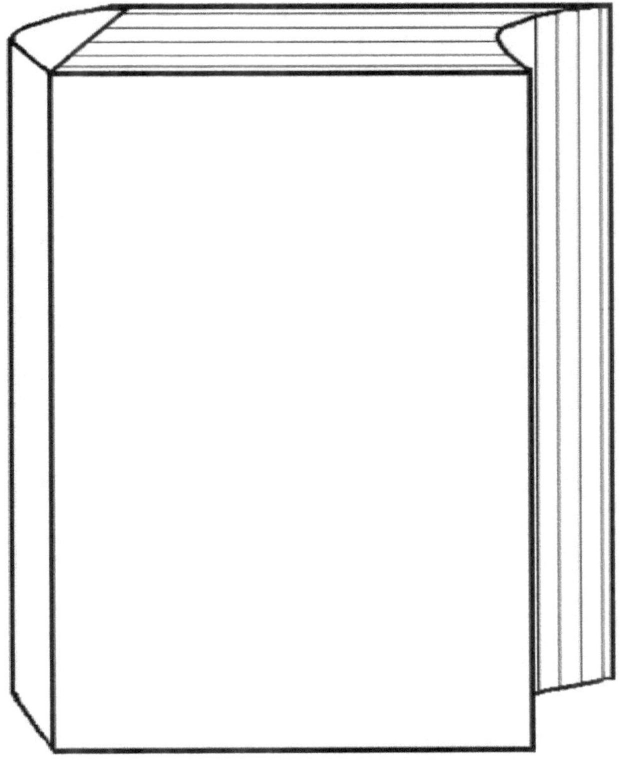

Licking Gently

Crystal blue sparkling water,
topped with white foam.
Licking gently the warm sandy beach.

Date Written 9/23/2020
1 Place ~ Verse

My Love Skates

Every Saturday I loved going skating,
all week that special day kept me waiting.
My dad would drop me off and pick me up,
always in my hand a cool water cup.
Each week I rented my skates,
it was less than pieces of eights.
One day my dad said just wait,
I did not know he would be so very great.
He came out with a skate box in hand,
he had this all well planned.
I opened the skate box up,
I felt like a new born pup.
A box filled with love,
my new skates fit like a glove.

Date Written: 8/25/2020
4 Place ~ Rhyme
Note: This is a true story. I was eight years old.
My dad was the best.

Roses Of Pink

R oses of pink are for me
O n this stem I do look and see
S weet smells you can breathe
E yes love pink roses for free

T he thorns will hurt
H ere I protect my stem skirt
O h red blood will squirt
R un a knife down so you will be unhurt
N ow enjoy without a flirt

Date Written: 7/5/2020
4 Place ~ Acrostic Rhyme

My Car

My car hit the ice
I have done it twice
cars watch out
now don't pout
I have no advice

Date Written:12/28/2020
5 Place ~ Limerick Rhyme

My Daddy

My
daddy
a great man
gave all he had
we loved him greatly
he gave his love
we enjoyed
daddy
bye

Date Written: 6/6/2020
3 Place ~ Ninette

Wearing Lime For Easter

Birds are singing it is Easter time.
What do I wear for this special date.
I see my outfit in color lime.
Flowers on fabric in groups of eight.
A pretty lacy wide brim lime hat.
Pink roses stand up no laying flat.
Dressed to the nines with churches closed.
Here reading my bible all composed.

Date Written: 4/8/2020
Honorable Mention ~ Rhyme

Here I Sit In My Nest

Here I sit in my nest,
eyes opened wide,
sitting looking out all stressed,
going to see if I can find a guide,
good to know you will pass the test,
do you want to be my bride?

Date Written: 4/17/2020
3 Place ~ Rhyme

Finding A Treasure In The Sand

As I walk the sandy beach,
a sea shell my hand will reach.
Wash it off in the blue water,
to give to my daughter.
A chain I found under a rock,
I will wear it with my smock.
I found treasures for my daughter and for me,
now let's go eat some crackers and brie.

Date Written:3/26/2020
Honorable Mention ~ Rhyme

The Crazy Neighbor

The neighbor down the street from me,
always had her polka dotted curtains open for all to see.
Music was playing loud,
there was a beat to that crazy sound.
When she walked out you never knew what you would find,
the colors she would wear could make one go blind.
Her five inch heels,
must have been made out of steel.
To top of her head,
a hat made out of bread.
She is one in a million,
or maybe that is one in a zillion.

Date Written: 3/16/2020
Honorable Mention ~ Rhyme

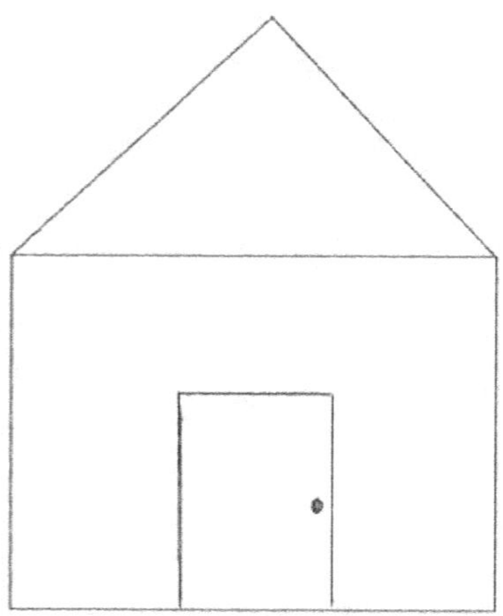

Many Friends

In life we have many friends.
Some friends are wonderful.
A few friends are great.
You started out as a friend.
You then moved quickly to a wonderful friend.
You now are a great friend.
All friend are priceless.
A great friend is worth their weight in gold.
Thank you for being my great friend.

Date Written: 3/12/2020
Honorable Mention ~ Free Verse

A Mother's True Love

Love comes in many shapes,
sizes and thoughts,
the love of flowers, things, our best pets.
Love may come as that special gift,
the one gift I have wanted or
may have been waiting for.
Love is given and received freely by some,
yet required by others.
Love by a Mother cannot be measured,
it is always free flowing.
Love gives up a loved child,
a child that needs to be cared for.
A Mother's True Love knows what is best
for her new baby,
love is a kiss to a baby that is never forgotten.

Date Written:1/25/2020
Third Place ~ Free Verse

The Cake Journey

A garden wedding is about to take place,
a lemon cake is requested.
A lemon cake should be easy to find,
lemons are a spring's delight.
A soft white frosting must be the cakes new dress,
no hard chewy frosting to get stuck in the teeth.
The cake journey is taking me to many cake shops,
no~no way~cannot do~is all I am hearing.
What is a friend suppose to do,
all I need is one lemon wedding cake dressed
with soft white frosting.
At the start it all sounded so easy,
a nightmare it has become.
What am I to do,
what will I tell the bride.
She is counting on me her maid-of-honor,
her lemon cake I must show up with.
The cake journey will continue,
I must find this lemon cake with soft white frosting.
I need to find it very soon,
this cake journey needs to end with a happy bride.

Date Written: 3/21/2022
3 Place ~ Dramatic Monologue

The Cake Journey Ends

A beautiful spring day wedding with big bees,
the sun is shining~birds singing~love
is in the cool breeze.
A lemon cake had been requested by the
bride on her knee,
soft white frosting to dress the cake in for all to see.
A spring garden wedding takes place
under the big shade tree,
she wanted plenty of pretty flowers~please.
I found a pretty yellow china rose it would not freeze,
a pretty pink rose made of china not cheese.
A lemon cake made with real lemons
and grated lemon skin,
soft white heavenly light frosting
to dress the cake in.
The cake journey has ended with a rhyme,
now for the two love birds it is honeymoon time.

Date Written: 4/26/2022
4 Place ~ Rhyme

My Blue Dinosaur Nursery Rhyme

You are a friend of mine,
we can run-play and make a rhyme.
Why is everyone afraid of you,
you are just big-soft and blue.
Blue Dinosaur we can play all day,
we can make you out of clay.
Now to sleep so say goodnight,
I will hold you ever so tight.
Off to dreamland,
so we can play in the sand.

Date Written: 3/6/2021
1 Place ~ Nursery Rhyme

I hope you have enjoyed my
"Nursery Rhymes and More."

Feel free to pass these "Nursery Rhymes"
and information on to others.
Below, you will find some information.
Thank You, for being one of my many readers.
Have A Great and Blessed Day Reading Away, Paula

The Adventures of Baby Cuz
"The Family"

My 1st Book in a Series of 3 Children's Books

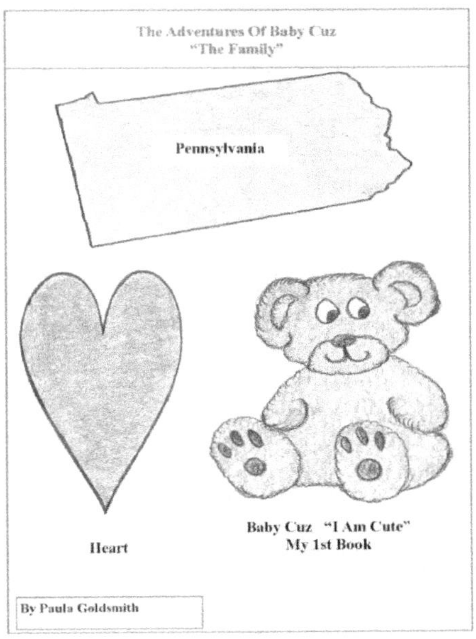

In this book "The Family," Baby Cuz experiences his third birthday. Your child will learn what makes Baby Cuz an adventurous little bear. The adventures are a fun way for children to learn about real life. They will also learn to read, spell and bring out their creativity and imagination as they "Personalize Their Book." There are "My Art Work" pages, for their art. Baby Cuz, is cute and he is told he is cute. That is why he says, "I am Cute." My son spent many loving hours with his stuffed bears, Baby Cuz and Uncle Fred. Uncle Fred is a real character. Throughout the books, Baby Cuz and Uncle Fred are the best of friends and love each other very much. Makes a great gift for all gift-giving occasions and holidays. When the child has outgrown the Baby Bear Books, they become a Great Keepsake for the Mother. Ages 2 and Up.

"What The Readers Are Saying" ~~And~~ "Reasons The Readers Are Loving These 3 Bear Books" Can Be Found Here At The End Of The 3 Bear Books

The Adventures of Baby Cuz

"Happy and Sad"

My 2nd Book in a Series of Children's Books In this book "Happy and Sad," Baby Cuz experiences his emotions of being happy and sad. He learns what happens when rules are not followed. The pages in each book were designed to be black and white. The child can color in the pictures as they learn words. Their personal Baby Cuz book will become very special to each child as they learn along with Baby Cuz. When the child has outgrown the Baby Bear Books, they become a Great Keepsake for the Mother. Ages 2 and Up.

The Adventures of Baby Cuz
"A Trip to Arizona"

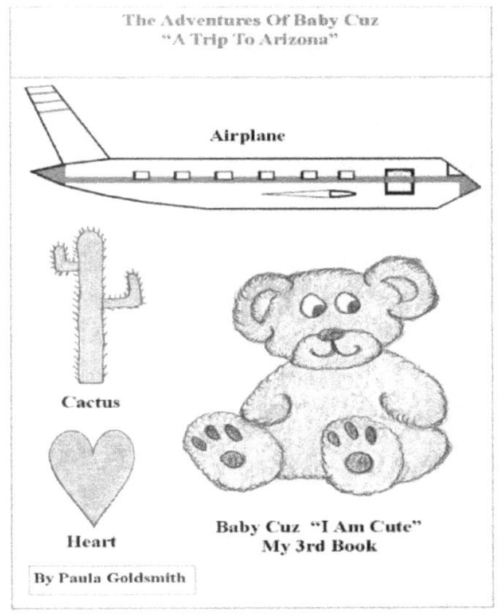

My 3rd Book in a Series of Children's Books In this book "A Trip to Arizona," Baby Cuz experiences his first airplane ride to visit his Uncle Fred who has retired in Arizona. Baby Cuz learns what makes Arizona an unique state. This book is great for children living or visiting Arizona. The bears take a trip around the state stopping and learning as they go. Since each child is an individual, no two books will be the same. Their personal Baby Cuz book will become very special. Uncle Fred is a big chocolate brown bear. He has traveled to many places and has a love for life. Baby Cuz is the cutest little bear. Watch for more books in this series of Baby Cuz. When the child has outgrown the Baby Bear Books, they become a Great Keepsake for the Mother. Ages 2 and Up.

What The Readers Are Saying About
"The Adventures of Baby Cuz's 3 Books"

1. Baby Cuz's adventures are interesting and fun for children and can help them learn about life and their surroundings. Sit down and grab a book and enjoy! From a Newspaper Editor.

2. Young readers will certainly enjoy this book while reading it or listening to it being read to them. They will learn valuable lessons. Youngsters will certainly grasp the lessons more quickly when given them by Baby Cuz, a Bear, than from other sources. Paula has done a great job of writing something children can enjoy, & at the same time, learn important lessons.
From an Author and Teacher

3. I am hooked!!! I cannot wait to read the next adventure of Baby Cuz. This new series of children's books are very refreshing.
A great way to learn. From an Author

4. I am Impressed with this book. It is an excellent way for you to help children learn to read and write. From a Mother, Grandmother and Author

Reasons The Readers Are Loving
"These 3 Bear Books"

1. Brings out Creativity and Imagination.
2. Personalize your Book.
3. A Story Book. My Art Work Pages. Learn to Read and Spell.
4. "Coloring" will bring your book to life. Coloring Book.
5. "Bear Tea Time." Juice and Cookies.
6. Makes a Great Gift for All Occasions, Holidays, the Sick, or the Shut-ins.
7. Easy to Mail in a Mailing Envelope.
8. Great when traveling. Make boring times like the airport, on the plane, car rides or a rainy day just fly by. The perfect place for recording all about your wonderful trip and what the child has learned.
9. Makes a Great Gift and Keepsake for the Mother when the child has outgrown the book/s. "Also" Great When Traveling. A Travel Keepsake. Add photos when you get home.

Have You Ever Heard An Angel Speak ?????

It seems adults have lost their creativity and imagination in this fast-paced world. This book of Beautiful Poems was born, to help bring back what we once felt when we were young. The book was designed for all ages. Ages 10 to 110 (many 7, 8, and 9 year old's love this angel book). You may want to add to your Personal Book with the blank pages in the back "Journal." Write your notes, dreams, and thoughts. If someone is sick, it is a great way to record the illness and recovery. If someone is in Hospice. The book makes a great keepsake for the family. Seniors will Love to make a Memoir Book or Family Recipe Book and Give it to Family Members. Traveling can be boring by car, in the airport, on the plane or a rainy day. This book is fun for the boring travel times. Journal all about your trip as a travel keepsake. Add trip photos. Adult Coloring Book." Bring your book to life with color, relax, de-stress and re-energize. The reader brings out their Creativity and Imagination as they Personalize their Book. Slow down and enjoy what God has given you. Be thankful for what you have and see the blessings that are all around you. How fun is it to have an "Angel Tea Time." The tea time can be very simple with

just tea and cookies, a luncheon tea time, or a banquet tea time.
This is a great way for a few ladies or a group to get together,
laugh, and have fun as they relax, de-stress and re-energize. An
angel tea time can be a great new funding-raising idea for a group.
Angels are loved all year long. (Christmas/Holiday Angel,
Valentine's Day Angels, Spring Angels, Mother's Day Angels,
Mother/Daughter Angels, Summer Time Angels, Thank You,
Angels/Volunteers). Great For Fund-Raising Events.
This book makes a very special gift for all occasions, holidays,
sick or shut-in. Books are easy to mail in a mailing envelope.
Check Out The "Angel Tribute" Page To Read What The Readers
Are Saying.   www.PaulasStories.com

"What The Readers Are Saying"

1. As Paula says, "take time, to make time, to laugh." I am getting
a couple of books for my friends. We are now going to spend our
lunchtime with an angel. What a refreshing and Inspiring book.
A must-have. From a Writer

2. Awesome Paula! We all need to be reminded that angels are all
around us. I am totally impressed with what you have done.
From an Author and Grandmother

3. We can be an angel to someone or someone can be an angel to
us when we need them the most. One can read the book for
inspiration. Thanks for giving us the opportunity to write down
our thoughts or to bring out our feelings as we draw like we did as
a child. What a concept! From an Author, Mother and Speaker

4. It is a nice piece of work. Very uplifting reading. Re-enforces
our beliefs of angels in heaven and on earth. From an Author and
Grandmother.

5. For Christmas, I received this wonderful angel book. It is great
and I love it. It is very different. I will get some for gifts. A gift
from a friend.

6. In the hospital, I got 4 adult coloring books. Your angel book
is the best. I love reading your poems. I love coloring the pages. I
love journaling about my illness and recovery. It has been a real
blessing to me. Thanks Paula

"Reasons Readers Are Loving This Angel Book"

1. Brings out Creativity and Imagination.
2. Personalize your Book.
3. A book of Beautiful Poems with a Journal section.
Write your thoughts, say what you want to say.
4. Your joy of "Coloring" will bring your book to life.
Adult Coloring Book.
5. "Angel Tea Time." What a fun way to spend some time with friends and escape from life for an hour or two. Let's sip a cup of tea with cookies, laugh, read poems and do some coloring.
What A Way To Go, De-stress and Re-energize.
6. Students, Mothers, Working Women, Seniors. Ages 10 to 110, many 7, 8, and 9 years old's also love this book.
7. Makes a Great Gift for All Occasions, Holidays, the Sick, or the Shut-ins.
8. Easy to Mail in a mailing envelope.
9. Great when traveling. Make boring times like the airport, on the plane, car rides or a rainy day just fly by. Personalize your trip in the Journal section. The perfect place for recording all about your wonderful trip. Add your trip photos.
10. Makes a great gift for the sick. Gives the sick person three different options, read, write, or color. They can track their illness and recovery.
11. Seniors will Love to make a Memoir Book or Family Recipe Book and Give to Family Members
12. An Angel Tea Time is great for small and large groups or fund-raising events. Angel tea time can be very simple with just tea and cookies, an Angel tea luncheon, or an Angel tea banquet.
13. Angels are loved and are good all year long.
(Christmas/Holiday Angels, Valentine's Day Angels, Spring Angels, Mother's Day Angels, Summer Iced Tea Time Angels, Say Thank You to The Angels/Volunteers.)
14. "Angel Tribute" A Special Gift For Your Special Angel. A Special Keepsake. Great For A Birthday, Anniversary, Retirement, Funeral, Grief, and More. Great for a Pet lover.

HURT Personalize Your Book

This Unique Book, "HURT Personalize Your Book," is a series of short stories about "HURT." You may find yourself in one of the stories or learning from it. The Reader can Personalize their Book with Their   Name and through a Journal Section with Their Thoughts. Say what they want to Say. Write Your Hurts. Bring Your book to life with Color. Makes a Great Gift. A Great Way to Say, "I am sorry." In the book Write a note or Text on the Phone, "I Am Sorry." Let The Book Do The Talking For You. "I am Not a doctor and I do Not pretend to be one."
Ages 12 to 110. Younger ages may learn and joy from this book.

"What The Readers Are Saying"

1. It is beautiful and true. Good work Paula. From An Author
2. I must say I am impressed with your writing. From A Reader in Canada
3. Tremendous Potential. It's what happens to everyone. It would help many people know they are not the only ones going through whatever. From A World Traveler
4. It's Beautiful. I can relate. I can understand. From A Reader
5. I am ordering books to give out. From A Reader
6. Your book cell phone is genius. From A writer
7. Love all of your unique books. From A writer
8. What a new way to say sorry or to talk again. From A Reader
9. Everyone needs this book. From A writer

"Reasons Readers Are Loving This HURT Book"

1. Great Way to Say, "I am sorry."
2. You may learn from one of the stores.
3. Journal Section for writing.

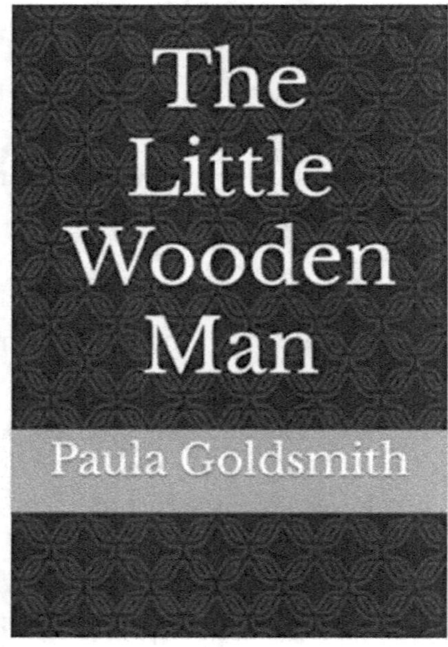

The Little Wooden Man is about three misfit kids that become best of friends. Their story of adventure takes you through their thick and thin as they are growing up. Can they solve the mystery of The Little Wooden Man??? Can you??? Only time will tell....... Ages 16 to 110 Younger ages may joy this fun book.

"What The Readers Are Saying"

1. Wow! What An Awesome Novel. From A Reader
2. Could Not Put This Down. From A Writer
3. This Maybe Your First Novel But Hope It Will Not Be Your Last. From A Reader
4. Your Creativity Is Really Amazing. From A Writer

"Award-Winning Poems"

Paula has been Honored to have her poems chosen to be printed in International Books of Poetry. In 2020 my poem, "When I Was Young" was Featured in "PS: It's Poetry A Brilliant Poetry Anthology Book." An International Book of Poems By International Poets. In 2021 a Children's Book, "Nursery Rhymes & Stories from Poets Around the World," was written by many International writers. She had "five" of her Nursery Rhymes chosen for this wonderful International Children's Book. In 2022 she had three poems chosen for this amazing book, "PS: It's Poetry A Brilliant Poetry Anthology Book Volume ll."

Read For "Free" Award-Winning International Poems on her website. Paula has Won over 200 Awards for her International Poems. At the bottom of each poem, it will say if it is a winner and what it has won. Check Out www.PaulasStories.com

What My Readers Are Saying About My Poems"

1. I love how all your poems tell a story. From A Reader
2. Your poems are so cute, clever, and creative. Keep writing your amazing poetry. Thank You
3. You are so creative. You have a talented and creative pen to write with. From A Writer
4. Your thoughts illuminate me. I love what you write. Thank You
5. When are you writing a book of poems? From A Reader
6. Keep writing your amazing poetry. I love reading it. From A Reader

Many of my readers have been asking me to publish a book with my Award-Winning International Poems. Here it is. This book only contains some of the hundreds of my Award-Winning International Poems. At the bottom of each poem will be listed what the poem won. This book is very different from my other six books.

This unique book **"Award-Winning Poems By International Poet Paula Goldsmith"** is a Fun book for Ages 10 to 110. In the back of the book, you will find a place to try writing your own poems. If you prefer you can journal about life. Make sure you bring your book to life with color. This book makes a Great Gift throughout the year. I hope you will enjoy this fun book and will pass it on to others to enjoy. Check Out www.PaulasStories.com

**Award-Winning Poems
By International Poet
Paula Goldsmith**

"Reviews"

1. Another great book. I love your amazing poems. From A Reader

2. Paula, you have wonderful creativity. A wonderful book for

gifts. I am ordering a few. From A Reader

3. Another Wow!!!! What a beautiful book of poems.

From A Reader

4. I read through it, then went back through this fun book.

Now off the bring it to life with color. From A Writer

5. I hope you will write a part two book. From A Reader

6. This book shows your amazing creativity. From A Writer

7. I love coloring my books to life. My kids love your kid's books.

Your books are so much fun for all ages. From A Reader

8. Some of your poems are very funny. I laughed until I cried.

From A Writer

9. Paula, you are a very talented and a gifted writer. From A Writer

10. Your fingers and poetic mind always produce amazing poetry.

From A Writer

"Don't Let Books Become A Thing Of The Past."

Read One Today For "FREE." Free E-Books ~ On Website.
Read for "Free" over 200 Award-Winning International
Poems ~ On Website.
Personalize Your Unique Book, Bring Out Your Creativity and
Imagination.
Paula has been Featured in over 18 Newspaper articles.
Books Are Internationally Sold.
"Please," Check Out: www.PaulasStories.com

I am so proud and humbled for the readers who took the time and
wrote a review. My readers are truly the best and I love each one
of them.

Again, Thank You, Paula